Original title:
Depths of Dreams

Copyright © 2024 Creative Arts Management OÜ
All rights reserved.

Author: Evelyn Hartman
ISBN HARDBACK: 978-9916-90-600-2
ISBN PAPERBACK: 978-9916-90-601-9

Inside the Enchanted Abyss

In shadows deep, where secrets sleep,
A whisper calls, through ancient halls.
The stars align, in dreams we dine,
With echoes faint, of love's restraint.

A tapestry of night unfolds,
With silver threads, and tales retold.
We dance with fate, in whispered grace,
Embracing all, in this timeless space.

The Lure of Unfathomable Horizons

Beyond the waves, where silence braves,
The horizon bends, where daylight ends.
A distant song, where we belong,
Calls out to hearts, with gentle starts.

The sunlit paths, through shadows cast,
Awaken dreams, where hope redeems.
With each step taken, fears awaken,
Yet courage gleams, in daring themes.

Dreamscapes of the Waking Mind

In realms of thought, where time is caught,
Visions arise, beneath blue skies.
Colors blend, where fancies send,
The whispered sighs, of sweet goodbyes.

With every glance, comes forth a chance,
To touch the stars, and heal our scars.
In dreams we tread, where hopes are fed,
The waking world, a canvas swirled.

The Abyss of Unseen Echoes

In depths profound, where lost words sound,
A haunting breath, whispers of death.
With shadows cast, the die is passed,
In silence reigns, the heart's old chains.

Yet in the dark, a fleeting spark,
Awakens fire, ignites desire.
In echoes lie, the reasons why,
The soul takes flight, beyond the night.

The Uncharted Waters of Thought

In quiet depths where shadows blend,
Ideas drift like boats unmoored.
Waves of doubt and hope extend,
Each thought a treasure yet to be explored.

Through storms of fear, the mind does steer,
Chasing dreams both bright and gray.
The compass spins, yet still we steer,
Finding peace in the fray.

Flickers of Forgotten Fantasies

In twilight's glow, the memories dance,
Whispers soft like twilight's sigh.
Once vivid dreams now lost by chance,
Flickers of light that dare not die.

Each shadow holds a story spun,
Of worlds we built with childlike glee.
Though time may age, the heart still runs,
In fantasies that set us free.

A Journey Through the Ether

Through silent realms where starlight flows,
We wander paths unseen by most.
Each breath a step as daylight slows,
In ether's grasp, we seek the lost.

Echoes call from realms apart,
Soft whispers trace the cosmic seam.
With open hearts, we play our part,
In the journey woven from a dream.

Murmurs from the Hidden Depths

In caverns deep where secrets sleep,
Murmurs rise like ancient tides.
Each echo holds a promise steep,
In shadowed nooks, our truth abides.

With every step, the darkness stirs,
Strange wonders mix with silent fears.
Through whispered depths, curiosity purrs,
As we unearth the buried years.

Floating Vignettes of the Heart

In whispers soft, the moments glide,
Through open roads where dreams reside.
Each fleeting glance, a tale untold,
Shimmering visions, brave and bold.

A dance of light on water's edge,
Reveals the secrets that we pledge.
With every heartbeat, stories dart,
Floating vignettes of the heart.

Beneath the starlit, vast expanse,
Life's gentle winds, they sway and dance.
In every sigh, in every part,
These tender notes pull us apart.

Yet still we dream, with souls in flight,
Embracing shadows, chasing light.
In every moment, we depart,
To find the truth within the heart.

The Enigma of Wandering Clouds

Above the world, they drift so free,
In silent forms, a mystery.
They twist and turn, a fleeting thought,
A sunset hue, a daylight caught.

The whispers of the sky unwind,
A canvas vast, where dreams are blind.
In shadows cast, they lose their shape,
Imprints of time, a soft escape.

A journey held by winds that sway,
As sunlight fades to twilight gray.
Each whispered breath, a hidden shroud,
The enigma of wandering clouds.

They gather hope, and then they part,
With every drift, they touch the heart.
In every storm, they paint our mood,
A tapestry of solitude.

Gossamer Threads of Illusion

In whispers soft, the dreams take flight,
Gossamer threads woven through night.
Fleeting visions, a dance of fate,
Trapped in shadows, we contemplate.

Wandering souls in twilight's embrace,
Chasing reflections, lost in space.
A tangled web where secrets lie,
Unraveling stories in a sigh.

The heartbeats echo in silent streams,
Painting the canvas of fragile dreams.
With every breath, a spark ignites,
Illusions shimmer, fading from sights.

Yet in the twilight, hope remains bright,
A golden glimmer in endless night.
For within the maze of what we feel,
Gossamer threads may just reveal.

The Uncharted Waters of Rest

Beneath the waves, the silence hums,
The weary heart in stillness drums.
Drifting softly on currents vast,
In uncharted waters, dreams are cast.

As shadows dance with gentle grace,
Time slips away in this sacred space.
Resting eyes upon the deep,
In whispered depths, the soul can leap.

Hidden treasures lie beneath,
In the quiet depths, we find relief.
Anchored hopes and tranquil minds,
In stillness, truth is what one finds.

So let the currents lead us far,
Where peace and calm are the guiding star.
In the uncharted, fears are blessed,
And in these waters, we find our rest.

Celestial Murmurs in the Dark

In the hush of night, whispers roam,
Celestial murmurs beckon us home.
Stars twinkle like secrets shared,
In the dark, wonders are declared.

The moon spills silver on paths unknown,
Guiding hearts to a place they've grown.
Every shadow dances with light,
Illuminating dreams that take flight.

With every breath, the universe sighs,
In cosmic embrace, the spirit flies.
Galaxies spill their ancient lore,
In hushed tones, they call for more.

So listen close to the soft sweet song,
In the dark where we all belong.
For among celestial whispers, we find,
Connections woven, body and mind.

Enigmas Wrapped in Starlight

Wrapped in starlight, secrets unfold,
Enigmas lie in patterns bold.
Twinkling visions, like velvet skies,
Holding mysteries where wonder lies.

With every star, a story spun,
Echoes of ages, lost and won.
In shadows cast by the night's embrace,
We search for meaning in this vast space.

The universe whispers, soft and low,
In riddles of time, it starts to glow.
Through every challenge and every test,
We find ourselves in the quest for rest.

So let us wander 'neath cosmic streams,
Chasing the shadows of unspoken dreams.
For in the depths of night's own flight,
We unearth enigmas wrapped in starlight.

The Mirage of Slumbering Realities

In shadows deep, illusions play,
Veils of dreams, they dance and sway.
A world adorned in silent whispers,
Echoes of hope, fleeting twisters.

Beneath the stars, we seek the light,
Through endless paths that fade from sight.
The mind awakens, yet still we roam,
In realms of wonder, far from home.

Fragments drift like scattered leaves,
Each thought a tale that gently weaves.
Reality bends, a curious sight,
As night embraces the fading light.

In slumber's hold, we find our grace,
In mirage worlds, we find our place.
With every sigh, the dreams combine,
A tapestry of the heart's design.

Rainbows Between the Mind's Eye

A spectrum bright, the thoughts do swirl,
In quiet corners, colors unfurl.
Each hue a whisper, soft and low,
Painting dreams in a vibrant glow.

Through whispered winds, the colors rise,
Chasing shadows beneath the skies.
A world unseen, where visions bloom,
In silent places, dispelling gloom.

Reflections dance upon the stream,
Where hopes arise like fragile dreams.
With every glance, the futures gleam,
A canvas woven from our theme.

In fleeting moments, let it show,
The rainbows born from the mind's glow.
In every heartbeat, life anew,
A bridge between the old and true.

In the Depths of a Whimsical Slumber

Where dreams do weave, a playful art,
In tender realms, we drift apart.
The night unfolds with gentle grace,
As time gives way to a hidden space.

In whispers soft, the fancies rise,
With laughter echoed in the skies.
Each slumbered wish, a secret kept,
In magical worlds, where none have slept.

Wings of hope take flight at night,
Across the void, they spark delight.
The depths reveal a cherished lore,
Adventures dance on twilight's floor.

With every sigh, the heart's embrace,
In whimsical paths, we find our place.
The morning beckons, yet still we cling,
To slumbering dreams and the joy they bring.

The Soundtrack of Sinking Thoughts

In echoes deep, the silence speaks,
A melody of the heart's soft peaks.
Each note a breath of what's confined,
A symphony of the restless mind.

As shadows stretch, the feelings churn,
In currents vast, the soul does yearn.
The whispers blend, a haunting tune,
While twilight dances with the moon.

Resonant waves through darkened skies,
In every heartbeat, a compromise.
The soundtrack plays, a bittersweet,
As sinking thoughts find their heartbeat.

From silence born, the music flows,
A cadence of what the spirit knows.
In timeless echoes, we shall find,
The haunting song of the drifting mind.

Reflections in the Ocean of Thought

In the depth, the shadows play,
Waves of ponder drift away.
Silent whispers, secrets deep,
In this realm, where thoughts do sleep.

Ebbing moments, tides of time,
Carried forth, like whispered rhyme.
Rippling echoes call my name,
In this sea, none are the same.

Glimmers bright, beneath the wave,
Truth and dreams, the heart can save.
Navigating through the haze,
Finding light in murky bays.

At horizon's edge we gaze,
Beneath stars, in silent praise.
Every thought, a droplet small,
In this ocean, I find all.

Floating Through the Fabric of Night

Stars adorn the velvet sky,
Moonlight weaves as shadows sigh.
Drifting where the dreams reside,
On the breeze, our hopes abide.

Thread by thread, the night unfolds,
Whispered tales from ages old.
Every twinkle holds a story,
In the dark, we seek our glory.

Dances of the night ignite,
Embers glow in soft twilight.
Floating dreams, a gentle spin,
In this fabric, we're akin.

As dawn breaks with tender light,
All our fears take flight from sight.
Through the night, we've soared so high,
Floating on, we kiss the sky.

The Mystique of Slumber's Embrace

In gentle arms, the night surrounds,
Where quiet peace and dreams abound.
Whispers soft, in shadows play,
As the world fades far away.

Cocooned in warmth, I drift and sway,
Stars invite, as thoughts decay.
In this realm, both vast and deep,
All my worries softly sleep.

Mysteries in darkness weave,
Beneath the quilt, our hearts believe.
Every sigh, a tale unfolds,
In the night, where silence holds.

Awake we'll find the break of day,
But in dreams, we wish to stay.
Slumber's spell, a sacred trance,
In her arms, we dream and dance.

Visions in the Twilight Hour

When daylight fades, the colors blend,
A canvas vast, where shadows send.
Twilight whispers, secrets shared,
In this hour, all hearts are bared.

Fading light, a painter's touch,
Drawing forth a world as much.
Every hue, a story told,
In twilight's grasp, we break the mold.

Time stands still as moments flow,
In the dusk, our visions grow.
Every sigh, a fleeting spark,
Guiding us through the coming dark.

As the sun bids soft goodbye,
In twilight's arms, we learn to fly.
With every breath, we chase the dream,
In this hour, everything gleams.

Beneath the Surface of Nightmares

In shadows deep where whispers dwell,
The haunting echoes weave their spell.
A dance of fears, a silent scream,
Within the dark, we lose the gleam.

Beneath the surface, secrets lie,
Twisted visions never die.
A world of dread that pulls us in,
With every battle lost within.

Face the specters, feel the chill,
In every heartbeat, linger still.
The night unveils our hidden plight,
As we traverse through endless fright.

Yet in this dark, a spark remains,
A hope that fights through boundless chains.
Awake we crave the morning's light,
To shed the weight of endless night.

A Journey Through Silvered Clouds

A silver mist, a shimmering sea,
Through boundless skies, where dreams float free.
Beneath the stars, we take our flight,
On gossamer threads woven with light.

Each breath a gust, each thought a sail,
Drifting softly on the celestial trail.
With every turn, a story blooms,
In the quiet, where magic looms.

The journey winds through realms unknown,
In silvered clouds, we find our home.
With hearts alight, we follow the muse,
In this ethereal realm, we choose.

Together we soar, through dreams so bright,
On paths of wonder, kissed by night.
Each moment a treasure, each sigh a song,
In this dance of twilight, where we belong.

Reveries of a Wanderer in Dreamland

In twilight's grasp, I drift away,
To lands where wishes softly play.
A wanderer's heart, a curious soul,
In dreamland's arms, I find my whole.

Mountains rise with whispers sweet,
Each step a tune, a rhythmic beat.
The rivers flow with secrets old,
In their embrace, I feel consoled.

Beneath the moons, the shadows dance,
In the woven light, I take my chance.
With every pulse, the visions grow,
A tapestry of dreams to show.

In reverie's hold, time stands still,
A world alive, a vibrant thrill.
As dawn approaches, I hold the key,
To dream once more, to set me free.

Under the Canopy of Sleep

Beneath the veil of midnight blue,
We drift away, the stars in view.
Under the canopy, soft and deep,
A world unfolds within our sleep.

With every sigh, the shadows play,
In gentle hues that fade away.
The moonlight bathes us in its grace,
As dreams unfold, a warm embrace.

In quiet realms where silence weaves,
The heart releases like fallen leaves.
A journey shared in whispered tones,
In slumber's lap, we find our homes.

As dawn arrives, the dreamers wake,
But in our hearts, the magic stays.
Under the canopy, love runs deep,
Forever cherished, who we keep.

Tides of the Unconscious

Waves crash softly on the shore,
Whispers linger from days of yore.
Dreams float gently on moonlit streams,
Hope and sorrow weave through our schemes.

Memories dance in twilight hues,
Hidden shadows cast by our views.
Emotions ebb and flow like the tide,
In night's embrace, secrets abide.

A pulse of life within the dark,
Each heartbeat sings, a silent lark.
In the silence, the depths unfold,
Stories untold in the folds of old.

Drifting on currents undefined,
We seek the truths we hope to find.
Through the depths, we will explore,
Tides of the mind, forevermore.

Labyrinths of Forgotten Visions

In winding paths, the lost ones stray,
Whispers of visions, faded and gray.
Each corner turned reveals a clue,
In shadows deep, the past breaks through.

Echoes of laughter, forgotten screams,
Dreams entwined in fragmented seams.
Searching for light in shrouded halls,
Hopes entwined within ancient walls.

Mirrors reflecting what could have been,
Glimpses of fate, tangled within.
In the heart of the maze, we ascend,
To find the light at the journey's end.

Through twisted routes, we learn to tread,
In the silence, new paths are bred.
With every step, the past unwinds,
Labyrinths hold what truth unwinds.

The Silence Between the Stars

In the vastness, quiet drifts profound,
Sparkling silence, no earthly sound.
Each star whispers a tale untold,
In the embrace of the night, we behold.

Galaxies dance in ethereal grace,
Time stands still in this timeless space.
Hearts beat softly in cosmic trance,
As we ponder the universe's expanse.

Connections bloom in the darkened void,
Memories shared, moments enjoyed.
In the stillness, our spirits soar,
The silence holds secrets forevermore.

With every flicker, hope ignites,
Guiding us through the infinite nights.
Between the stars, we find our way,
In celestial quiet, we choose to stay.

Chasing Phantoms of the Mind

In the corridors of thought we chase,
Phantoms swirling in a timeless space.
Whispers of fears, echoes of dreams,
Fleeting glimpses, or so it seems.

Shadows flicker, elusive and sly,
In the depths of the mind, passions lie.
Cascades of color, emotions collide,
In the dance of the psyche, we confide.

Through veils of darkness, we seek the light,
Chasing the phantoms that haunt the night.
With every heartbeat, we yearn to find,
The truths hidden deep in the fabric of mind.

A journey within, where chaos reigns,
A tapestry woven with joy and pains.
In the chase, we discover our soul,
Chasing phantoms, we become whole.

Driftwood of the Imagination

Waves wash dreams upon the shore,
Driftwood whispers of tales once more.
Murmurs of time in the salty air,
Fragments lost, yet always there.

In the stillness, thoughts do float,
Crafting stories, a silent boat.
Each piece of wood, a journey spun,
Carried away, then left undone.

Hearts wander far, like birds in flight,
Painting visions in fading light.
A canvas bright with colors bold,
Renewing hopes, a sight to behold.

Secrets swim in the ocean deep,
Where dreams are sown and silence keeps.
In the tides of thought, free to roam,
Driftwood guides our way back home.

The Chasm of Lost Reveries

In shadows cast by faded youth,
Lie echoes of forgotten truth.
A chasm yawns, wide and deep,
Where dreams once soared in silence sleep.

Whispers linger, soft and low,
Winding paths where lost thoughts go.
Memories dance on the edge of night,
Flickering hopes that flicker out of sight.

The heart does ache for what was gone,
A melody sweet, now just a song.
Fragile visions in twilight fade,
Embers warmth of dreams displayed.

Yet in the dark, a spark remains,
The echo of joy still entertains.
Bridges built from the void we feel,
Reveries wait, their wounds to heal.

Secrets of the Sleeping Soul

Beneath the veil of midnight's shroud,
Whispered secrets gather loud.
In tranquil realms where visions sleep,
The soul holds truths both vast and deep.

Gentle dreams on silken threads,
Weaving tales where silence spreads.
Each heartbeat a soft lullaby,
Taking flight, through starlit sky.

Haunted whispers softly call,
In the stillness, shadows fall.
Moments hidden, treasures rare,
Awakening, we find them there.

In slumber's grip, the spirit sings,
Unlocking joy that healing brings.
The mysteries in us unfold,
Secrets cherished, silently told.

Beneath the Canvas of Night

Stars are scattered like painter's brush,
In darkness deep, the night does hush.
Whispers of dreams in the chilly air,
A tapestry woven with utmost care.

Beneath the cloak of twilight's grace,
Shadows dance in their own embrace.
The moon paints silver on sleeping streets,
A lull of magic in heartbeats.

The world slips softly into a trance,
Where silence beckons the mind to dance.
Each twinkle a promise, a fleeting glance,
Awakening wonder in night's expanse.

Wrapped in stillness, our spirits soar,
In dreams and wishes, we seek for more.
Beneath the canvas, life takes flight,
Chasing stars through the velvet night.

The Surreal Journey of a Silent Night

In shadows deep the whispers play,
The stars above begin to sway,
Underneath the moon's embrace,
Time stands still in this still space.

A path adorned with silver dreams,
Where nothing's ever as it seems,
Each breath a song, a lullaby,
To wander through this endless sky.

The night unfolds a tapestry,
Of secrets held in silent glee,
With every step a story spun,
In realms where fear and hope are one.

Embrace the quiet, let it flow,
In this surreal and soft glow,
The journey lingers, never ends,
A night as vast as time extends.

Portraits of Shade and Light

In corners where the shadows dwell,
Light dances sweetly, casts its spell,
Each brush of color paints the air,
A portrait drawn with tender care.

Through every hue, a story lives,
Of joy and pain that daylight gives,
The shades of life, both dark and bright,
Create a world of pure delight.

A gentle hand can shift the gaze,
From proving ground to golden phase,
In contrast lies the beauty found,
In fleeting moments all around.

With every stroke, a truth ignites,
In the portraits of our days and nights,
For in the blend of shade and light,
We find our path, our guiding sight.

Through the Looking Glass of the Night Sky

Beneath the veil of sapphire dreams,
The cosmos whispers, softly gleams,
Through glassy eyes we gaze above,
A universe that's filled with love.

Constellations, stories old,
In patterns bright, their tales unfold,
Reflecting hopes, our fears, our fights,
In the looking glass of starry nights.

Each twinkle born from distant light,
Calls gently to the heart's delight,
To ponder paths where stardust flows,
And maps the secrets heaven knows.

So wander forth with open mind,
Through the vast sky's embrace, you'll find,
In every star, a spark divine,
A glimpse of truth, forever shine.

The Secret Garden of the Mind

In quiet corners, thoughts abound,
Where wildflowers of dreams are found,
A garden blooms within the heart,
With every seed, we claim our part.

The whispers of forgotten lore,
Invite us in to seek much more,
Among the shadows, colors blend,
Creating worlds that never end.

With every breath, the petals sway,
As visions dance and drift away,
Each moment spent here feels so free,
In the secret garden of the mind's decree.

So nurture hope, let worries cease,
In this domain we find our peace,
For every thought, a flower grows,
In this enchanted garden's prose.

The Chiaroscuro of Night Terrors

In shadows thick, the silence creeps,
Whispers draw near, as the darkness leaps.
Figures dance in flickering light,
A haunting waltz in the depths of night.

Eyes wide open, yet I cannot see,
Lurking thoughts, they reside in me.
Each heartbeat echoes, a thunderous sound,
In the chiaroscuro, I'm tightly bound.

Memories merge with the formed regrets,
Living nightmares that time forgets.
Dreadful beauty in the fear so stark,
A canvas painted dark, yet marked.

But dawn will break, the night will fade,
A subtle shift, the terror laid.
Chiaroscuro shifts in the morning's embrace,
Revealing the truth, a softening grace.

Harvesting Stars from the Darkness

From midnight's hold, I seek to claim,
Twinkling jewels, each one a name.
They whisper stories with ancient might,
Harvesting dreams from the endless night.

With every breath, I gather light,
Casting nets in the cosmic flight.
Celestial treasures in the void's expanse,
Each star a chance, each flicker a dance.

Cradling hopes that hope to be,
A galaxy's pulse beats inside of me.
From shadows deep, my spirit soars,
Harvesting stars, forever explores.

In solitude's grasp, I find my way,
Across the heavens, brightened sway.
Though darkness lingers, it cannot snuff,
The brilliance born from the times so tough.

Treading on Twilight Pathways

As day surrenders to nightfall's kiss,
Twilight whispers, a moment of bliss.
Where shadows merge in soft descent,
I tread on pathways, twilight spent.

With every step, the world grows dim,
Colors fade, the edges slim.
A bridge between the here and there,
In twilight's arms, I find my care.

Silhouettes wander, echoes in flight,
Faint glowing orbs, a shimmer of light.
Mysteries blend, both near and far,
As I tread softly, beneath the stars.

The dusk holds secrets, too shy to share,
Yet in its depths, we find the rare.
Treading on pathways where dreams ignite,
Embracing the magic of the coming night.

The Dialogues of Fleeting Visions

In the silence, visions clash,
Echoes linger, a silent thrash.
Fleeting whispers, stories collide,
In the twilight's realm, they never hide.

Words unspoken, yet loudly felt,
In the gallery where shadows melt.
Every glance a tale unfolds,
The dialogues whisper, the heart beholds.

Chasing shadows, I weave and bend,
Through corridors where spirits send.
Glimmers of truth in the half-light seem,
A tapestry spun from the threads of dreams.

When dawn approaches, the visions part,
Leaving traces, a gentle chart.
The dialogues linger, won't disappear,
Fleeting echoes of what we hold dear.

The Symbiosis of Night and Thought

In shadows deep, ideas flow,
The night ignites a brilliant glow.
Whispers dance on silken air,
Creativity blooms, laid bare.

Stars above, a guiding light,
Mingling dreams with the quiet night.
Thoughts entwined in cosmic grace,
In this realm, we find our place.

Moonlit paths, where secrets hide,
Silent musings, our hearts abide.
Each moment a chance to explore,
In the stillness, we find our core.

As dawn creeps in, shadows flee,
Yet night's embrace will always be.
A symbiosis, forever fine,
Where night and thought, together, shine.

The Veil Between Two Worlds

A curtain drawn, a whisper's breath,
Living lightly, flirting with death.
Echoes linger in twilight's grace,
Two worlds meet in a sacred space.

Time stands still, as visions blend,
Where dreams and reality transcend.
Ghostly figures dance in the mist,
What is lost, but not forgotten, kissed.

Eyes wide open, hearts prepare,
To tread the line between despair.
Bridges forged on the edge of night,
Guided softly by inner light.

With each step on this fragile seam,
We learn to exist in both realms' dream.
The veil lifts gently, soft and rare,
Two worlds merge in the silent air.

Glimmers of Hope in the Murky Abyss

In depths where shadows twist and curl,
A flicker shines, as dreams unfurl.
Hope's soft whisper cuts through the dark,
Guiding souls like a tiny spark.

Murky waters, a maze of fear,
Yet against despair, light draws near.
Each heartbeat echoes, strong and clear,
Resilience born, we learn to steer.

Through the depths, we find our way,
Shining bright at the break of day.
Glimmers spark in the thickest night,
A testament to our inner fight.

In the abyss, we rise and see,
The path ahead, a mystery.
Clutching hope, we boldly press,
Refusing to succumb to distress.

The Enchantment of Unraveled Slumber

In dreams where the wildflowers grow,
Woven tales begin to flow.
Unwrapping layers, soft and light,
As slumber beckons through the night.

Enchantment fills the air so sweet,
Where reality and fantasy meet.
A dance of shadows, whispers call,
In this haven, we will not fall.

Each thread of night, a story spun,
As stars align, we come undone.
Awake to wonders, let them bloom,
In the fading light, we embrace the loom.

Through midnight's gate, we gently glide,
In dreams we trust, where hope resides.
The enchantment lies in dreams we share,
In unraveled slumber, free from care.

Tides of Unseen Realms

Waves that whisper secrets deep,
In shadows where the mysteries sleep.
Currents pull the heart's desire,
To places where the dreams conspire.

Oceans swirl with ancient lore,
Guiding souls to distant shore.
In the depths, the echoes call,
A journey binding one and all.

Ripples dance under moonlit skies,
Cradling hopes in softest sighs.
As the tides begin to rise,
Awakening the world's surprise.

Unseen realms that shift and sway,
Invite the brave to find their way.
In the magic of the night,
They sail toward the unseen light.

Beneath the Surface of Slumber

In dreams where shadows softly sway,
The mind's eye wanders, far away.
Beneath the veil of night's embrace,
A hidden world, a secret place.

Whispers float on silken threads,
Through the silence, softly spreads.
Secrets held in every sigh,
As the stars weave stories high.

Time stands still as visions bloom,
In the depths of nocturnal gloom.
Below the surface, shadows play,
A dance that pulls us to stay.

Awake or asleep, the lines blur,
As dreams and night begin to stir.
In slumber's grip, we find our ground,
A universe where peace is found.

Labyrinths of the Night

Through winding paths where shadows creep,
A journey deeper, thoughts to keep.
Each corner turned, a choice to make,
In the dark, the fears awake.

Moonlit echoes guide the way,
Igniting worlds where phantoms play.
Footsteps echo, soft yet bold,
In whispers of the stories told.

Heartbeats quicken, senses heighten,
In the maze, the doubts grow frightening.
Yet courage flickers like a flame,
Through labyrinths, we seek our name.

Finding light in every turn,
The night's embrace, a place to learn.
In the depths where shadows chase,
We carve our path, we find our place.

Beneath the Starlit Mirage

Underneath the vast expanse,
Stars twinkle with a distant glance.
Mirages dance in silver light,
A fantasy that grips the night.

In dreams of sky and whispered breeze,
Hope ignites beneath the trees.
Each constellation tells a tale,
Of love and loss, a cosmic trail.

The night unfolds, a canvas wide,
Where secrets shift and shadows hide.
Every wish cast into the air,
Is treasured deep, beyond compare.

Beneath the starlit, shimmering glow,
The heart of dreams begins to flow.
In this mirage, the world stands still,
Awakening the soul's sweet thrill.

Fragments from the Land of Nod

In slumber's grasp, the dreams do weave,
Whispers soft, in twilight's eve.
Colors dance on velvet air,
Fragments lost, yet somehow there.

A gentle sigh, the moonlight glows,
Secrets kept, where no one knows.
Stars align in patterns vague,
Promises in shadows, they beg.

Through wisp of fog, the echoes rise,
Past fading thoughts, like fireflies.
Scattered tales on stardust trails,
Each story flows where silence sails.

In this realm where visions drift,
Time is but an artful gift.
Awake to find what heart recalls,
A tapestry of dreams enthralls.

Cradled in the Embrace of Shadows

In twilight's cloak, where silence sings,
The world retreats, on quiet wings.
Beneath the stars, a soft embrace,
Shadows dance with supple grace.

Whispers thread through ancient trees,
Carried forth on gentle breeze.
Cloaked in night, our secrets lie,
Hidden truths beneath the sky.

Eyes of dusk, they watch and gleam,
A tender lull, a fleeting dream.
Within the dark, our spirits soar,
Cradled safe, forevermore.

Embraced by night, fear fades away,
In shadow's fold, we'll always stay.
Together bound, we find our way,
To dawn's soft light, a brand new day.

On the Edge of Luminous Dreams

At the horizon where wishes tread,
Luminous paths where visions spread.
A dance of light in midnight's grasp,
Holding dreams in daylight's clasp.

Between the stars and shadows cast,
Glimmers of hope, bright and vast.
In the silence, a heartbeat calls,
To venture forth where wonder sprawls.

Tender glows in the heart of night,
Each flicker a promise, pure and bright.
On edges frail, the mind takes flight,
In painted skies, we chase the light.

With every breath, the colors swirl,
In cosmic dance, we twirl and whirl.
On the edge where dreams ignite,
We find ourselves in purest light.

The Hidden Tides of Reflection

In rippling pools, where thoughts collide,
The hidden tides of time abide.
Mirrored faces, fading grace,
Captured moments we embrace.

Waves of memory ebb and flow,
Carrying seeds of long ago.
In quiet depths, the heart can see,
Reflections of what used to be.

Voices whisper through the glass,
Revealing tales of future, past.
In stillness found, we ponder deep,
The secrets of the soul we keep.

With every glance, a world unfolds,
In hidden tides, the truth beholds.
Floating dreams on currents wide,
We journey forth with hearts as guide.

The Vessel of Forgotten Wishes

In a chest of dust and dreams,
    Whispers linger, lost it seems.
    Wishes curl like fragile leaves,
Time forgot what the heart believes.

    Shimmering in twilight's gaze,
    Hopes entwined in shadowed haze.
    Each secret casts a fleeting glow,
    In the vessel, time moves slow.

    Echoes of what might have been,
    Lurking deep, a silent din.
    Heartfelt murmurs, soft and bright,
    Yearning for the lost daylight.

    Let the current take them free,
    Into the vast, uncharted sea.
    For every wish that fades away,
    New ones spark, a bright array.

Veils of the Subconscious

Beneath the layers of thought's deep sea,
Hidden dreams wait patiently.
Veils that shroud the waking mind,
Secrets linger, hard to find.

Shadows dance in silent halls,
A whisper fills the empty walls.
Memories drift like autumn leaves,
In the stillness, the spirit weaves.

Like shadows cast by flickering light,
They play tricks both day and night.
Truth and illusion intertwine,
In the depths where thoughts align.

Lift the veils, let visions soar,
Explore the depths forevermore.
For in the mind's enchanted place,
We find our truth, our hidden grace.

Echoing through the Nebula

Stars whisper tales of ancient lore,
Cosmic echoes forevermore.
Through the depths of endless night,
Dreams take wing, purest light.

Nebulas swirl in colors bright,
Cradling secrets in their flight.
Celestial symphonies resound,
In the silence, beauty found.

Each heartbeat a pulse of space,
Time itself begins to trace.
Echoes blend in harmony,
A dance of fate, forever free.

Journey on, where wonders gleam,
Follow the path of a distant dream.
For in the vast, the soul will sing,
To the stars, our hearts take wing.

The Subtle Currents of Desire

In the hush of a moonlit night,
    Longing flows, soft as light.
    Currents twist in tender grace,
    Pulling hearts to a secret place.

    Gentle whispers, fleeting touch,
The dance of souls, it means so much.
    An electric brush ignites the air,
    In the stillness, passions flare.

    Waves of silence rise and fall,
    A longing deep, we can't recall.
With every glance, a spark ignites,
The subtle dance of hearts' delights.

Dive into the currents, lose control,
Let desire guide the wandering soul.
    For in its depths, we find our way,
    In longing's grip, we wish to stay.

Navigating the Waters of the Imagination

In the depths of thought, we dive,
Sailing on waves that come alive.
Mysteries whisper through the air,
Guiding us to places rare.

The horizon shifts with every dream,
Life flows like an endless stream.
Colors dance and shadows play,
In this realm where wishes sway.

Charting paths 'neath starlit skies,
Unlocking worlds with open eyes.
Each stroke of thought, a vivid hue,
Creating landscapes rich and new.

Casting nets of hope and light,
Navigating through the night.
With every turn, we find our way,
In the waters of dreams, we stay.

Luminescence in Lush Constellations

Beneath the velvet cloak of night,
Stars whisper softly, pure delight.
Each twinkle holds a tale untold,
In galaxies where dreams unfold.

The moonlight bathes the world below,
In silver threads, like gentle flow.
Rippling through the tranquil air,
A dance of light, beyond compare.

Celestial paths we trace in thought,
With every flicker, wisdom brought.
Infinite wonders in our sight,
Guiding hearts with gentle light.

In this expanse where shadows blend,
Cosmic currents never end.
We weave our hopes with every gaze,
In lush constellations, we are praised.

Curiosities of the Sleepwalker

In the stillness of the night,
Dreamers roam in soft moonlight.
With hesitant steps, they glide and sway,
Lost in visions that lead astray.

Whispers echo through the air,
Guiding souls with gentle care.
Curiosities flourish and bloom,
In the quiet, shadows loom.

Eyes half-closed, they wander free,
Dancing where the mind can see.
Every heartbeat, a silent song,
In the realm where dreams belong.

Each step a story, spun in flight,
Curious hearts embrace the night.
With every breath, the world expands,
In the grips of sleep's gentle hands.

Dreams Entwined with Reality

In a world where visions blend,
Dreams and waking moments mend.
Threads of gold in twilight's seam,
Stitch together what seems a dream.

Moments linger, hand in hand,
Blurring lines where thoughts expand.
Reality softens, takes a flight,
Illuminating the darkest night.

With each heartbeat, dreams take form,
Riding waves of thought, a storm.
Weaving tales both rich and rare,
Entwined in magic, we find our air.

As dawn breaks and shadows fade,
Echoes of dreams, serenely played.
In the tapestry of night's embrace,
We find the truths we long to trace.

Echoes Lost Among the Stars

In the night where whispers dwell,
Faint echoes of a distant bell.
Stars twinkle with secrets of old,
Stories of dreams and hearts untold.

Wanderers trace their paths in light,
Hoping to find a guide through night.
Lost memories drift in the breeze,
Embraced by shadows of ancient trees.

The cosmos sings a haunting tune,
Beneath the watchful eye of the moon.
Each twinkle holds a silent plea,
To grasp the moments that longed to be.

Yet in the vastness, still we yearn,
For the flickers that once would burn.
Echoes fade, but hearts still fight,
To reach the stars that spark the night.

Grappling with Shadows of the Soul

In the corners of a silent mind,
Shadows linger, hard to find.
Fighting battles, dark and deep,
In the silence, secrets keep.

Voices whisper, doubts arise,
Reflections caught in hidden lies.
Grappling with the weight of fear,
Yearning for light to draw near.

Moments shatter like fragile glass,
Each cut reveals the scars we amass.
Yet in the struggle, hope can bloom,
Casting light amid the gloom.

Facing shadows, we gain our might,
From darkness, emerges the light.
A journey within, fierce and whole,
To embrace the depths of the soul.

Beyond the Horizon of Sleep

When the world fades to a sigh,
And dreams take wing, we learn to fly.
Beyond horizons, free we roam,
In lands where fantasy feels like home.

Whispers of stars in twilight's embrace,
Guiding us to a timeless place.
Each slumber holds a tale to weave,
In the web of what we believe.

Fields of wonders, oceans of light,
Where every shadow dances in sight.
Awake and asleep, we intertwine,
Chasing visions, both yours and mine.

Beyond the horizon, dreams unfold,
A tapestry of stories untold.
In the twilight, we find our keep,
Embracing the magic beyond sleep.

The Allure of Boundless Landscapes

Mountains rise like ancient stone,
Calling to those who roam alone.
Valleys stretch with arms wide,
Inviting hearts to seek and bide.

Rivers dance beneath the sky,
Whispering secrets as they flow by.
Fields of gold, horizons swirl,
An endless canvas, a painter's pearl.

In the quiet, the wild calls,
Breathing life as nature sprawls.
Wonders bloom where trails entwine,
The allure of landscapes divine.

With each step, the spirit sings,
In the presence of wings and things.
Boundless beauty, forever anew,
In nature's heart, we find the true.

Whispers Beneath the Veil

In the hush of dreams, they speak,
Voices soft, yet full of weight.
Secrets tangled in the night,
Moonlit paths where shadows wait.

Beneath the veil of silver mist,
Gentle hands weave tales untold.
Each breath a story, each sigh a wish,
In whispers shared, our hearts unfold.

The stars align in sacred dance,
Echoing thoughts we dare not share.
In the silence, there's a chance,
To find our truth, laid bare and rare.

So let us linger, just a beat,
In the shadowed corners of our mind.
For in the whispers, love is sweet,
A bond unbroken, gently signed.

Shadows of the Midnight Mind

In the dark where thoughts converge,
Beneath the veil of moonlit sighs,
Shadows dance and dreams emerge,
A tapestry where silence lies.

Flickers of light, the mind's parade,
Echoes trapped in dreamy eves.
Each wave of thought, a spectral braid,
In the stillness, the heart believes.

Whispers traced in midnight air,
A lullaby of fears and hopes.
In shadows cast, we find the rare,
Life's mysteries entwined with ropes.

So linger here, in thoughts divine,
Let the midnight clarity unwind.
For in the chaos, we may find,
The hidden truth our souls designed.

Echoes in the Twilight Abyss

In twilight's grasp, we hear the call,
Echoes dancing on the breeze.
Lost whispers rise to softly fall,
Where light and shadow dare to tease.

Beneath the sky painted in dreams,
The abyss cradles our quiet fears.
In every breath, the silence schemes,
A depth of solace, void of tears.

Voices linger, timeless and free,
Reflecting on the paths we've tread.
In the void, a mystery,
Where thoughts unite, and hearts are fed.

So cast your worries to the night,
Embrace the echoes, let them guide.
For in the twilight's fleeting light,
Our souls find peace, forever tied.

Navigating the Silent Sea

Sailing through a sea of dreams,
Where silence reigns and echoes play.
Each wave a thought, or so it seems,
Guiding our hearts on the endless sway.

Beneath the stars, the compass glows,
Charting courses, we drift along.
In stillness, the mind's river flows,
Creating worlds where we belong.

The quiet depths hold treasures rare,
Glimmers of truth within the dark.
In silence, we find what we dare,
A whispering light, a radiant spark.

So launch your vessel, free and bold,
In the silent sea, let love be found.
For in the depths, life's truths unfold,
A symphony of hearts, profound.

Gazing into the Pool of Night

Stars shimmer like gems, lost in the deep,
Reflections of wishes, secrets we keep.
The moon whispers softly, a lullaby sweet,
Embracing the silence where shadows meet.

Clouds drift like whispers, tales yet untold,
Drizzling moonlight on dreams made of gold.
In this tranquil moment, the world fades away,
Just the night and I in an endless ballet.

Ripples of starlight dance on the face,
Carrying echoes of time and of space.
Gazing intently at the vastness above,
My heart beats softly, cradled by love.

In the pool of night, I find my refrain,
A sanctuary serene where the soul breaks its chain.
Each twinkle a promise, each sigh a release,
In this quiet cosmos, I discover my peace.

The Ethereal Dance of Dreamweavers

Under the veil of the twilight's embrace,
Dreamweavers gather in a mystical space.
With threads of the night and whispers of light,
They spin into being the visions of flight.

Each dancer adorned in a shimmer of stars,
Creating enchantments that travel afar.
With gentle movements, they beckon the mind,
To wander in realms where the heart feels unconfined.

Silken dreams flutter like petals in air,
Inviting the dreamers to join in their fare.
With laughter and joy, they weave vivid schemes,
Unraveling stories, igniting our dreams.

As dawn breaks the spell and the dancers depart,
The magic resides deep within every heart.
In the glow of the morning, we cherish the night,
A tapestry woven in shimmering light.

Silver Lining of the Sleepy Sky

The sleepy sky blankets a world filled with dreams,
Soft whispers of starlight, gentle moonbeams.
Clouds drift like memories, calm and serene,
Painting the horizon in shades of routine.

Colors of twilight blend warm with the cold,
The silver lining glimmers, a promise untold.
As day surrenders to the kiss of the night,
Hope dances softly in the fading light.

In moments of stillness, the magic unfolds,
Revealing the beauty that quietness holds.
Each star a reminder, a spark from above,
Lighting our pathways with comfort and love.

With dreams in our hearts, we gather and sigh,
Beneath the vast wonders of the sleepy sky.
In the glow of the twilight, we find our way,
Embracing the night as we welcome the day.

Puzzles Pondered in the Dark

In the quiet of night, mysteries awake,
Puzzles of shadows, illusions we make.
Thoughts swirl like smoke in a dimming light,
Searching for answers that elude our sight.

Each question a key to a door yet unseen,
Unlocking the riddles that whisper in between.
As stars wink in laughter, secrets play hide,
We ponder in silence with wonder as our guide.

The darkness conceals what the day cannot hold,
A canvas of queries, waiting to unfold.
With every heartbeat, the questions take shape,
Bringing forth visions that challenge and escape.

In the depths of the night where the mind roams free,
Puzzles of existence invite you and me.
In this labyrinth of thought, we dance and we dive,
Finding the answers that keep us alive.

Fragments of a Fading Illusion

In twilight's grasp, we lose our way,
Shadows linger where colors play.
Whispers of laughter fill the air,
Echoes of dreams dance everywhere.

Moments fracture like glass on stone,
Tales of yesteryear now overthrown.
Time's gentle hands, they warp and bend,
Leaving behind what we can't mend.

Eyes that sparkle, now dimmed by time,
Once bright with hope, now void of rhyme.
We chase the light, yet find it gone,
In the silence, we move along.

Yet in the fragments, stories gleam,
Lost in the hustle of life's cruel scheme.
We seek a solace in what we knew,
In fading illusions, truth breaks through.

Secrets Hidden Beneath the Pillow

Underneath the soft embrace,
Dreams and secrets find their place.
Whispers wrapped in twilight's shroud,
Hopes that shimmer, quiet and loud.

Pillows cradle thoughts untold,
Memories wrapped in threads of gold.
With every sigh, the night reveals,
A tapestry of heart's true feels.

Stars above, they silently gaze,
Guardian of our midnight phase.
What lies beneath that frayed seam,
Unraveled threads of every dream.

In solitude, the whispers speak,
A soft embrace for the strong and weak.
Beneath the pillow, life unfolds,
Secrets wrapped in comfort hold.

Tracing the Ineffable Paths

Across the canvas of the night,
We seek the stars that fade from sight.
Footsteps echo on timeless ground,
In silence, the universe resounds.

With every turn, a question grows,
In uncharted realms, truth flows.
Paths entwined with shadows vast,
Carrying whispers of the past.

Maps are drawn with fading ink,
In every step, we learn to think.
The heart remembers where to tread,
Tracing trails of words unsaid.

Yet every journey finds its close,
In cycles new, the spirit grows.
In ineffable moments, we explore,
Paths lead us back to what we sore.

The Silhouette of Lost Dreams

In corners dark, they gently sway,
Fragments of what we threw away.
Silhouettes dance in moonlit beams,
Haunted shadows of lost dreams.

Whispers swarm like autumn leaves,
Carried forth by nighttime thieves.
We clutch the past with trembling hands,
In the silence, our heart expands.

Every flicker tells a tale,
Of hopes that fading winds unveiled.
Yet in the dark, we find our way,
In silhouette, dreams refuse to stay.

But caught in dreams, we learn to soar,
Through the shadows forevermore.
In the dusk, we find our seams,
The beauty lies in lost dreams.

Untold Stories Beneath Heavy Lids

In shadows cast by dreams so deep,
Whispers linger where memories weep.
Silent secrets in the night unfold,
Tales of the brave, the lost, the bold.

Underneath eyelids, worlds take flight,
Dancing softly, far from sight.
Fables woven from strands of time,
Echoing softly, a silent rhyme.

In the depths of slumber's embrace,
Hidden truths find their rightful place.
With each heartbeat, stories entwine,
Ink of the soul, the heart's design.

Awake yet dreaming, the journey stays,
Journeying through the night's gentle maze.
Untold stories, in silence kept,
Beneath heavy lids, the heart has wept.

Cradled in the Arms of Night

Stars blanket the sky in a cosmic hug,
Holding the world, a soft, warm rug.
Moonlight spills like silver threads,
Cradling dreams in their gentle beds.

Whispers of wind through the trees sigh,
A lullaby sung as the day bids goodbye.
Crickets sing in a soft refrain,
A serenade sweet, without a chain.

Night wraps around like a lover's grace,
Every heartbeat slows, every worry misplaced.
In the embrace of the dark so vast,
Time drifts away, and shadows are cast.

Cradled within, the heart finds its light,
In the darkness, we learn to take flight.
The world outside softly fades from sight,
As we are held in the arms of night.

The Abyss Between Wakefulness and Sleep

A thin veil hangs, a delicate thread,
Between the alive and the softly dead.
Thoughts wander where silence reigns,
In the grey area where nothing remains.

An ocean deep, a still, quiet stream,
Caught in the balance of waking dream.
Fleeting moments flicker and fade,
Lost in the dance, in twilight's shade.

Here lies the realm of the nearly gone,
Where mind and body gently yawn.
In this chasm, all worries cease,
A pause in the world, a moment of peace.

The abyss calls softly, a siren's song,
Enticing the weary to linger long.
Between the two, a universe vast,
Curled in the arms of a future and past.

An Odyssey Through the Ethereal

Lifted by winds of a whispered tale,
We sail through dreams on a shimmering trail.
Stars our compass, the moon our guide,
In realms uncharted, we slip and slide.

Colors collide in a dance of grace,
Every heartbeat quickens, every breath a trace.
Through valleys of light, we wander and roam,
Finding our way, we weave through the gloam.

Echoes of laughter follow our path,
Woven with shadows, a gentle aftermath.
In the ethereal mist, our spirits find wings,
An odyssey calls, where the heart truly sings.

As dawn approaches, we hear the songs,
Of worlds that have waited, of belonging and throngs.
In the depths of this journey, forever we'll stay,
An odyssey through night, into the day.

Beyond the Surface of Reality

Beneath the veil of light we find,
Truths hidden deep, intertwined.
Each shadow tells a whispered tale,
Of dreams that rise and hopes that sail.

In quiet corners of the night,
The stars align, a wondrous sight.
We reach beyond what eyes can see,
Embracing depths of mystery.

With every heartbeat, wisdom grows,
A dance of fate that ebbs and flows.
To venture forth, we brave the storm,
In realms where shadows keep us warm.

So let us soar on wings of thought,
For in this quest, our souls are caught.
Beyond the surface, we explore,
The endless wonders, evermore.

Navigating the Cosmic Subconscious

In starlit dreams, our minds do roam,
Through galaxies far from our home.
Each heartbeat echoes in the dark,
A cosmic dance, a hidden spark.

Our thoughts like comets wildly blaze,
In timeless voids where silence plays.
We bridge the gap from flesh to light,
In whispers soft, we chase the night.

Navigating through the astral sea,
We find the truth of what we could be.
Each fragment shines with vibrant hue,
And in this quest, we all renew.

With every pulse, the infinite calls,
In boundless realms where starlight sprawls.
So let us venture through the skies,
And seek the wisdom that never dies.

Whispers Beneath the Surface

The water's edge, a quiet place,
Where secrets linger, time does trace.
In every ripple, tales unfold,
Of ancient love and fortunes bold.

Beneath the waves, the silence breathes,
In the shadows, the heart perceives.
Whispers of longing, soft and clear,
Resonate with all we hold dear.

The pulse of life beneath the skin,
In labyrinthine depths we begin.
With open hearts, we dare to dive,
In the embrace of dreams, we thrive.

So listen closely, take the chance,
In the depths of stillness, we dance.
For in the quiet, truths appear,
And whispers guide us, ever near.

Echoes in a Midnight Reverie

When twilight's gown drapes o'er the night,
And stars ignite their gentle light,
The echoes of the past resound,
In dreams where lost desires are found.

Each moment pauses, softly sways,
In midnight's grip, the heart displays.
A symphony of whispered dreams,
That flow like silvered, moonlit streams.

In reverie, the shadows bloom,
And time dissolves the endless gloom.
With every sigh, the memories sweep,
Into the depths of twilight's keep.

So let us wander through this space,
Where echoes linger, time's embrace.
In midnight's reverie, we find,
A tapestry of heart and mind.

The Palette of Sleepless Wanderers

In shadows cast by moonlit glow,
With colors deep, the night does flow.
Each brushstroke whispers tales untold,
A tapestry of dreams unfolds.

Wanderers roam with hearts ablaze,
In search of truth through misty haze.
Their spirits dance beneath the sky,
As stars ignite, their hopes will fly.

The palette spills, a canvas vast,
Where memories of youth are cast.
Each hue a moment, vibrant, bright,
In the sleepless wanderers' night.

Through streets unknown, with feet unbound,
They paint their dreams on solid ground.
With every step, their souls take flight,
In the palette of this endless night.

Reflections in a Dreamer's Eye

In twilight's haze, where visions blend,
A dreamer's eye seeks journeys' end.
Reflections dance like shadows wane,
In whispered dreams, there's joy and pain.

Mirrors cast in silver beams,
Reveal the heart's forgotten dreams.
Each glance unveils what lies beneath,
In silence blooms a world of wreath.

A flicker glows in starlit skies,
As hopes and fears in tandem rise.
The dreams they weave, a secret art,
Alive within a beating heart.

In the realm where fantasy flows,
The dreamer's eye forever knows.
With every blink, new worlds arise,
In reflections of a thousand skies.

Fleeting Thoughts in the Abyss

In the depths of night, thoughts softly tread,
Like whispers lost, in shadows spread.
They flit and flutter, brief as light,
In the abyss, they take their flight.

A moment's grace, a fleeting glance,
These thoughts entwine in cosmic dance.
They vanish swift, like smoke in air,
Leaving traces that linger where.

In silence deep, the echoes call,
Each fleeting thought, a rise, a fall.
They weave the fabric of our mind,
In the abyss, what will we find?

With open hearts, let them flow free,
These fleeting thoughts of you and me.
In the vast expanse, we search and seek,
In the abyss, our souls unique.

The Keepers of the Night's Secret

The stars align in silent watch,
As whispers thread through night's debauch.
The keepers guard what lies in dark,
With tender glow, they light the spark.

They cradle dreams in velvet hands,
While shadows dance on ancient lands.
Each secret bound in silver night,
Unfolds within the keeper's sight.

In moonlit glow, the stories flow,
Of love and loss, of joy and woe.
The keepers weave with gentle care,
A tapestry of secrets rare.

With every breath, the night confides,
In silence, where the magic hides.
They guide the lost, the brave, the meek,
The keepers of the night's mystique.

The Abyss of Slumbering Hopes

In the quiet folds of night,
Dreams lie still, out of sight.
Whispers of wishes, soft and low,
In the abyss where hopes do flow.

Glimmers fade like distant stars,
Beneath the weight of silent scars.
Yet somewhere deep, a spark ignites,
Yearning for the dawn's first lights.

Echoes linger in the mind,
Memories of what we hoped to find.
As shadows dance in gentle sighs,
We gather dreams from starlit skies.

Awakening from slumber's grasp,
To hold the dreams we dare to clasp.
The abyss calls to those who dare,
To rise and meet the morning air.

Beneath the Veil of Night

Beneath the moon's soft, silken glow,
Secrets whisper, hopes bestow.
Dreamers wander, lost in thought,
In the silence, solace sought.

Stars adorn the velvet skies,
Echoes of truth in gentle sighs.
Where shadows blend and darkness dwells,
Mysteries weave their sacred spells.

Time slows down, the world stands still,
Awakening a hidden thrill.
In the depths of night, we find,
A tapestry of souls entwined.

With every heartbeat, dreams ignite,
Fuelled by passion, fierce and bright.
Together we wander, hand in hand,
Beneath the veil, a promised land.

Drowning in a Sea of Fantasies

In a world where dreams take flight,
We drift along on waves of light.
Sacred visions, deep and vast,
In the sea of fantasies cast.

Waves crash down with a siren's song,
Pulling us under, where we belong.
Glimmers of hope on the surface gleam,
In this ocean, we dare to dream.

Treading water, we search for more,
Diving deeper to explore.
Hidden treasures in depths unseen,
Awakened hearts and souls serene.

With every breath, we swim anew,
Finding courage in what is true.
Drowning softly, yet we rise,
In a sea where the spirit flies.

Shadows of Unseen Realities

In the corners of a quiet mind,
Shadows move, subtly entwined.
Echoes of lives not lived yet,
In the recess where dreams are set.

Veils of reality float like mist,
Whispers of moments that we missed.
Every choice, a path we tread,
In the shadows where fears are fed.

But light breaks through, a hopeful beam,
Illuminating our deepest dream.
In shadows cast, we find our way,
Unseen realities, here to stay.

Awake, we lean into the light,
Embracing futures bold and bright.
For in the shadows, life reveals,
The truth of what our heart conceals.

Corteges of the Dusk Hour

Silhouettes on the horizon glow,
As the sun dips low and shadows grow.
In the quiet, secrets softly sigh,
Beneath the canvas of a dusky sky.

Footsteps echo, a gentle parade,
Memories dancing in twilight's shade.
Stars awaken, one by one,
To weave their dreams, as day is done.

Night unfolds its velvet cloak,
In whispered tones, the twilight spoke.
Time slows down, the world at rest,
In the hush, the heart feels blessed.

With each breath, the night draws near,
In the dusk, we release our fear.
Corteges of moments, fleeting and rare,
Embrace the dusk, in night's tender care.

Starlit Melodies of the Heart

In the quiet of the night, a song arises,
Soft as whispers, bright as surprises.
Notes cascading like dew from the stars,
Healing our wounds, soothing our scars.

Each melody dances, a silvery breeze,
Filling the soul with tranquil ease.
Underneath the moon's gentle beam,
Our hearts awaken, igniting the dream.

Harmonies linger, drifting like mist,
In the stillness, they can't be missed.
Starlit tunes wrapped in the night,
Guide us home with their tender light.

Together we sway, hearts intertwined,
In this starlit embrace, love is defined.
Melodies echo through the cool air,
A timeless bond, forever we share.

Skylines of Infinite Possibilities

Beyond the horizon, the skyline glows,
Painted with dreams that the heart knows.
Colors merging in a vibrant dance,
Inviting the soul to take a chance.

Each dawn reveals a canvas anew,
A realm of hopes, shimmering like dew.
In the sky's embrace, we dare to dream,
Chasing the light, like a golden beam.

Clouds drifting softly, tales to tell,
Of journeys taken and where we fell.
In the vastness, our spirits soar,
Skylines beckon, urging us to explore.

With every sunset, a promise is made,
To follow our paths, unafraid.
The sky whispers secrets, bold and bright,
In the silence of day, we find our flight.

Whispers of Tomorrow in a Dreamcoat

In the soft twilight, whispers arise,
Floating on breezes, under vast skies.
Wrapped in a dreamcoat of hopes untold,
Tomorrow's promise in threads of gold.

Each stitch a vision, woven with care,
A tapestry rich, beyond compare.
In moments of pause, we feel the embrace,
Of the future's adventure, its warm trace.

Dreams unfold like petals at dawn,
Unraveling paths that we can be drawn.
Through the fabric of time, we traverse wide,
With whispers of tomorrow as our guide.

In the stillness, listen and feel,
The flicker of dreams, the world reveals.
Tomorrow awaits in a dance of chance,
Draped in the glow of a hopeful glance.

Milton Keynes UK
Ingram Content Group UK Ltd.
UKHW022117251124
451529UK00012B/567